BOOK ANALYSIS

**Martian
Chronicles**

BY RAY BRADBURY

BOOK ANALYSIS

Written by Michel Dyer
Translated by Oliver Brown

Martian Chronicles

BY RAY BRADBURY

Bright
≣Summaries.com

RAY BRADBURY

AMERICAN WRITER

- **Born in 1920 in Waukegan, Illinois, USA**
- **Died in 2012 in Los Angeles, California, USA**
- **Some of his works:**
  - *L'Homme illustré* (1951), collection of short stories
  - *Farenheit 451* (1953), novel
  - *Theatre for Tomorrow... and Beyond* (1972), play

Ray Bradbury was a prolific writer who, from the age of 18, published short science fiction stories in fanzines (independent publications, often produced by amateur enthusiasts and aimed at other enthusiasts – hence the word "fan" made up of fan and magazine. The first ones appeared in the United States in the 1930s and were devoted to science fiction). Influenced by Robert Heinlein (American writer, 1907-1988), "dean of American science fiction" and master of the short story, he was the major figure of the genre during the 1950s, along-side Isaac Asimov (American-Russian writer, 1920-1992).

His committed and melancholic texts contrast with the major trends in science fiction of his time, which were sensationalism and comedy. He achieved international fame with *Fahrenheit 451*, which is still one of the best-known science fiction novels in the world, along-side George Orwell's *1984* (British writer, 1903-1950). Although his career did not enjoy the same success from the 1960s onwards, it is important to note that he is one of the few writers in the genre to have ventured into theatre and even poetry.

MARTIAN CHRONICLES

A FOUNDING CLASSIC OF SCIENCE FICTION

- **Genre:** *fix-up* (a collection of short stories arranged in such a way that they can be read together, like a novel)

- **Reference edition:** *Chroniques martiennes*, translated from English by Jacques Chambon and Henri Robillot, Paris, Denoël, 2001, 318 p.

- **1st edition:** 1946 (first short story), 1950 (first complete edition, renewed in 1977)

- **Themes:** Anticipation, space travel, war, colonialism, aliens

The Martian Chronicles are composed of about thirty short stories (their number has varied according to the editions; in the Denoël edition, there are 28) of very different lengths, the shortest being hardly more than one page, the longest exceeding thirty pages. This disparity can be explained by the very history of the book, which is a *fix-up*, i.e. the creation of a novel from a set of short stories with similar themes.

The longer stories were all originally published in magazine form and then reworked to fit the overall economy of the novel, while the shorter ones were written later to link the stories together and create coherence. The undeniable success of *The Martian Chronicles*, which tells the story of how, in the space of half a decade, man colonised and then abandoned Mars, led to an altered reissue in 1997: originally set between 1999 and 2026, the action of the novel was pushed back 31 years into the future, to avoid the so-called "future now past" problem, although this did lead to some chronological approximations.

SUMMARY

The Martian Chronicles are organised in three main parts, which can be broken down chronologically, as each story begins with a date in the form of a 'month + year'. From January 2030 (or 1999 in the original version – for the sake of consistency, we will refer to the dates of the revised edition) to August 2032, man's expeditions to Mars end in failure: it is the impossible conquest. Then, from August 2032 to November 2036, it is the terra-formation of Mars, its inexorable colonisation. Finally, from November 2036 to October 2057, it is the extinction of the human race following the war, and the establishment of Mars, almost deserted, as a new Garden of Eden.

The first two movements are therefore surprisingly abrupt: we see a new Martian expedition fail every six months, and then Man spread over the entire planet in less than five years; whereas the last movement comprises an ellipse of more than twenty years. The whole is not really a novel, but rather a series of chronicles. Indeed, each chapter, or short story, is self-sufficient, closed on itself, does not require a sequel and introduces characters who will not (except in exceptional cases) be reused. There is therefore no narrative scheme in *The Martian Chronicles*, but there is a definite historical sense – the removal of the assumed fictionality of the novel gives the *fix-up* a greater consistency.

The Martian Chronicles opens with an astonishing short story, the first in a series of failed First Contacts between human explorers and Martians, with the former being killed by the latter three times.

"Ylla" is the chronicle of a couple's life: the year is 2030, and Yll K. and Ylla K. are a more or less happily married couple – Ray Bradbury hints at the husband's infidelities from the wife's suspicious and naive point of view. They have 'the coppery skin, the eyes like gold coins, the delicately musical voice of real Martians' (page 22). The story uses a common but very effective science fiction device: the reversal of the point of view. The Martians are here the normal, familiar everyday people, and the humans are the invaders. This is one of the only stories in the novel to use Martians as the main characters, but it has an active effect on the following chapters: the reader sides with the Martians, who are shown to be subtle and in the right, while humans act as shameless invaders – and there is a playful aspect to this: the reader is surprised to guess how the expedition will fail and how the Martians will kill the humans.

The first eight short stories seem to establish a pattern: how man, once he arrives on Mars, sees his attempt at colonisation reduced to nothing. From the outset, the diversity of tones strikes the reader: in "The Men of the Earth", the fate of the Second Expedition is treated comically (they are thought to be mad, since the Martians, by telepathy, can impose the image of their madness, in this case human appearance, on others); that of the Third, in "The Third Expedition", alternates between melancholy and horror (the members of the Expedition are killed in their sleep by Martians who pretend to be their deceased relatives)

But suddenly, Ray Bradbury removes the Martians from the equation: they all die, or almost all die, leaving their planet empty. The novel then takes a completely different turn, and the short stories become much more heterogeneous. They are no longer variations on the theme of the man deceived and killed by the Martian. We meet a priest who tries to readapt Christianity to extraterrestrial life, a woman who is ready to leave all her earthly comforts to join her husband who whispers the word 'love' to her through interstellar space, but also the last Martian life forms, which bring men face to face with their loneliness and sadness.

Bradbury uses Mars as a huge science-fictional laboratory to tackle racial problems (an astonishing short story in which all the blacks leave deep, segregated America for the Martian El Dorado), the question of mourning or even that of censorship, a foreshadowing in the horror genre of the theme of *Fahrenheit 451*. He paints a global picture of the effects of a mass migration to Mars, questioning what would drive a human being to leave so far from home – the lure of gain, a quiet retreat, fear of war, boredom...

The last news item introduces an abrupt thematic change – with the war on Earth getting worse, the colonists unanimously decide to *return* to their planet. This choice, which does not immediately make sense to the reader, is particularly well captured by Bradbury, who has gone to great lengths throughout the story to emphasise the fact that humans could never feel at home on Mars. Longing for Earth would always be insurmountable, and nothing, ultimately, awaited them on the Red Planet. Better to die at home than to continue living on an alien planet after the extinction of one's species. The last human beings on Mars are the forgotten ones, the latecomers, who did not choose to remain alone and do not emerge unscathed from this terrible abandonment, driven mad by loneliness.

Nevertheless, the very last story presents a family consisting of the two parents and three young sons who narrowly manage to escape from Earth to Mars. What was presented to the children as a 'holiday' turns out to be the last chance for humanity, soon to be extinct on Earth. From being a new El Dorado, Mars becomes the new Garden of Eden.

CHARACTER STUDY

THE MARTIANS

This is obviously one of the curiosities of a science fiction novel set on Mars, one of the criteria by which the reader judges the book: how has the author imagined, shaped, singled out the Martians? *The Martian Chronicles*, by their specificity, offer multiple answers, and finally almost as many visions of the typical Martian as of individualized Martians, with variations from one novel to another. Nevertheless, certain recurring features can be identified: coppery skin, golden eyes, a kind of mask on the face and the use of telepathy. But even these recurring features can be undermined: in the short story "Nocturnal Encounter", the main character Tomás meets the ghost of a Martian (or maybe it's the other way around…) who speaks 'his own language'. Thus, during their first exchanges, "they did not understand each other" (page 135), and the Martian has to touch Tomás' head to learn, instantly, his language. If there is indeed a telepathic element at play here, note the discrepancy with a similar encounter between Captain Williams and the Martian Mrs Ttt, at the very beginning of the short story "The Men of Earth": "How is it that you speak our language so perfectly? – I don't speak, I think. Telepathy!"

The reader is somewhat confused: does the Martian then have a language or not? Bradbury often depicts him as a being capable of modifying the sensory perceptions of the beings around him by his very thought, up to the indefinable, forever changing being of the short story "The Martian", whom every human sees as the loved one he would like to see. But sometimes the Martian is also a being very close to man, as in the short story "Ylla", where the Martian couple resembles in every way the typical New York couple of the mid-20th century[e]. There are also other Martian races, such as the luminous balls that save the lives of men in danger and present themselves as evolved beings in the short story "The Fireballs". As we can see, Bradbury does not try to create a typical Martian who returns from story to story, but paints a mythological portrait of him, creating a legendary being, with blurred outlines, always mysterious to humans, elusive and incomprehensible.

THE MEN

For the most part, the human characters appear only for the space of a short story. Some, however, recur, or at least are mentioned in another story. These include Captain Wilder, Jeff Spender, Hathaway and Sam Parkhill, all members of the Fourth Expedition, whom we follow in the short story "… And the Moon That Shines", the real nodal point of the novel. Others, such as William Stendhal (in the short story 'Usher II') or Father Peregrine (in the short story "The Fire Balloons" are simply more prominent.

CAPTAIN WILDER

The central character of the short story "... And the Moon That Shines", he is the captain of the Fourth Expedition, the one that will find Mars emptied of its inhabitants, decimated by the terrestrial diseases brought by the previous expeditions. A sensitive but determined character, he resolves to shoot Spender for the greater good of the exploration mission, although he does not disagree with his ideas in substance. We find him twenty-five years and two hundred pages later in the novella "The Long Years": back from unsuccessful expeditions to Jupiter, Saturn and Pluto, he finds the planet empty of its inhabitants again, the men having gone back to Earth to die. He comes across one of the last survivors, Hathaway, one of the members of the Fourth Expedition, who dies in his arms. Once again, he shows great understanding for the actions of his former officer.

JEFF SPENDER

A member of the Fourth Expedition, he stands out from the others by his boundless admiration for Mars and the Martians: in particular, he falls in love with an abandoned city. Cultured and sensitive (he quotes a poem by the 19th century British poet Lord Byron), but also misanthropic, it is easy to see him as an alter ego of the author. After a disappearance in the form of a spiritual quest, he decides to avenge the Martians and kill those who desecrate their world – i.e. his former companions in exploration. He plans to trap and kill all future adventurers, thus unknowingly repeating the pattern of the early stories: the humans arrive, the Martians kill them. However, alone against all, he ends up being killed by his captain, Wilder, despite their friendship. His philosophy, which Wilder promises to defend, is nevertheless lost when it is learned that Wilder has been removed from Mars for political reasons.

HATHAWAY

He is the doctor-geologist of the Fourth Expedition, and it is he who decrees the death of all Martians because of chickenpox. He becomes the central character of the short story "The Long Years". Isolated for almost twenty years, he survived his family, decimated by the disease (tragic irony?). To overcome his loneliness, he has built androids that resemble them in every way, but he has not been able to make them age. When he dies, Captain Wilder decides not to deactivate the androids, recognising that they have a life of their own.

SAM PARKHILL

Another member of the Fourth Expedition, he is very vindictive towards Spender. According to Spender, he has all the American's faults. In the short story "The Off-Season", he is the recipient of the deed to Mars, which the last Martians give him. Without understanding that this deed is a sadly ironic gift, since the Martians know Earth is doomed, Parkhill leaps with glee, imagining the fortune he can amass by setting up hot dog stands and thus sadly echoing Spender's words ('The only reason we didn't set up hot dog stands in the middle of the Temple of Karnak was because it didn't offer lucrative enough prospects', page 96). However, as with all his characters, Bradbury does not condemn him entirely, and Parkhill like the others returns to Earth when the threat of the end of humanity becomes tangible.

WILLIAM STENDHAL

He is a wealthy lover of literature who has fled to Mars to escape the censorship, the 'naming of names' that is rampant on Earth, i.e. the censorship of vocabulary to expunge controversial words, such as 'politics' or 'escape'. But knowing that the censors would follow him to Mars, he plots his revenge by having the House of Usher, from the eponymous short story by Edgar Allan Poe (American writer, 1809-1849), reproduced. Assisted by the genius mechanic Pikes, he builds killer automatons and a booby-trapped house to decimate the elite of the 'Society for the Suppression of the Imaginary'. Bradbury first mentions the theme, which he will take up again, in a much more melancholic and pessimistic tone, in his masterpiece *Fahrenheit 451*.

FATHER PEREGRINE

He is a pastor who longs to go to Mars to discover new forms of sin, 'sins on another world' (p. 146). Presented as an unconventional and even eccentric churchman, doubted by his peers, he turns away from the colonists to deal with the souls of the Martians, although he is informed that they are on the verge of extinction. Eventually, he discovers some: beings in the shape of 'fireballs' that rescue humans in distress. Together with his companions, he builds them a church with a Christ in the shape of a balloon. However, the Martians come back to him to tell him that they have overcome their material condition and are free from sin. Father Peregrine is a complex character, through whom Bradbury criticises religion and mysticism, while at the same time recognising certain virtues. In particular, the character is highlighted for his unshakeable faith and ability to believe, very much like that of the science fiction fan.

READING KEYS

SCIENCE FICTION AS A TOTAL LITERARY GENRE

When *The Martian Chronicles* were published in 1950, science fiction was in the midst of a commercial golden age in the United States: it was the rise of the fanzines. However, the first masterpieces of the genre were still fairly isolated, and their authors were not American: let us mention *Brave New World* (1931), by Aldous Huxley (British writer, 1894-1963), *The World of Ā* (1945) by A.E. van Vogt (Canadian writer, 1912-2000) or even *1984* (1948) by George Orwell. In this sense, the year 1950 is a major date in the history of science fiction: it saw the publication of Isaac Asimov's *Robots* and Ray Bradbury's *The Martian Chronicles*, which stand out for their *fix-up* form and their founding way of making science fiction. In a universe that was already highly codified, but not yet recognised as such (note that the novels of Orwell and Huxley refute the label 'science fiction' and are, even today, often published in general literature collections), Asimov and Bradbury laid the foundations that influenced a whole generation of authors.

Like any reader of science fiction, the reader of *The Martian Chronicles* has to make adjustments of an encyclopaedic nature, that is to say, to locate in the text the clues that allow him or her to construct a system of functioning for the fictional world presented by the author. For the reader of today even more than for the reader of 1950, this adjustment takes the form of a ret-roactive game that is part of the generic architext of science fiction: each reader reads armed with the imagery associated with Mars and the colonisation of the Red Planet that he or she has already encountered, from *The War of the Worlds* (1898) by H.G. Wells (American writer, 1866-1946) to the film by Tim Burton (American director, born in 1958), *Mars Attacks!* (1996).

It is a question of reconstructing, little by little, with the help of the text, a specific vision of Mars and of the future imagined by Bradbury, with a deliciously old-fash-ioned taste. Anticipation and space travel are thus two of the sub-genres of science fiction that best lend themselves to the encyclopaedic work of the reader. One of the specificities of *The Martian Chronicles*, as we have seen with the cohabitation of different and even contra-dictory data on the Martians, is that it disrupts several times, within itself, this encyclopaedia in the making.

THE ARCHITECTURE

This literary concept was proposed by Gérard Genette (French literary critic, 1930-2018). Architextuality is one of the five forms of transtextuality that he devel-ops in his book *Palimpsests* (1982), along with inter-textuality (the presence of one text in another, notably through quotation), paratextuality (everything that surrounds the text, such as the notes), metatextuality (when one text comments on another) and hypertex-tuality (when one text parodies or copies another).

Architextuality is the relationship of a text to its genre and conventions, i.e. everything that makes it possible to perceive it as part of a literary genre - in this case, the mere fact that the action is set on Mars would be enough to make *The Martian Chronicles* a work of science fiction.

A fundamentally new aspect of the science fiction in *The Martian Chronicles* is the mixture of genres: the painting of manners, the horrific tale, the social pamphlet, the micro-stories… But within this mixture of genres lies a mixture of science fictional sub-genres: space travel and the encounter with an extraterrestrial intelligence, of course, but also robots and dystopia. As the various short stories are originally independent, they are not linked together by any unity of tone, theme or genre. Thus, the science fiction motifs are often only a background, a pretext, a way of introducing certain themes, and if the action did not take place on Mars in the 2030s, the text would no longer have much to do with the idea of the genre.

However, this would be to lose sight of the fact that science fiction is above all an extraordinary narrative instrument, more than a contextual one. By introducing a 'what if' situation, the novelist opens the doors of possibility wide. Thus, the mourning in the short stories "The Martian" and "The Long Years" is treated in a typically science-fictional way - the author introduces a paradigmatic change (if there were a form of life capable of imitating a departed being perfectly, or even too perfectly) and then questions its consequences, thus shedding new light on the subject.

Is it better to live alone with the memory of the loved one or with an ersatz that one knows to be a deception, but with an illusion so perfect that one wants to forget it? At first glance, the reader may dismiss this question as abstract and seemingly unrelated to reality, since it does not concern him or her and probably never will.

However, the literary validity of the process seems undeniable, and questioning through a new, albeit theoretical, lens provides results. It is, for example, by extrapolating the theme of family reunification beyond the conceivable that Bradbury best reflects on marital love – is there a fundamental difference between a woman leaving home to live with her husband and that same woman leaving her planet? Finally, science fiction is an easily suppressed narrative tool – one could transpose *The Martian Chronicles* in time and space – for example to America in the early 19th century[e] ...

AN ACERBIC RE-READING OF THE COLONISATION OF AMERICA

Ray Bradbury hardly hides this fact and even makes it explicit at several points: *The Martian Chronicles* do not tell the story of how man arrived on Mars, but how the American arrived on Mars:

> "The rockets were American, the men were American, and things stayed that way, while Europe, Asia, South America, Australia and

the islands watched the Roman candles go without them. [...] The second emigrants were still Americans" (page 143).

Throughout the stories, there is a comparison between the Martian world and the vast American plains, between the Martians and the American Indians, between the settlers from Earth and those who came to settle their European way of life on the American continent. The expression 'New World' is here literally updated by Bradbury.

The short story "... And the Moon That Shines" is in this sense one of the most remarkable of the *Chronicles*. It features an explorer, Spender, who, struck by the beauty of Mars and its abandoned cities, decides to kill all the other explorers to protect the planet forever from the ravages of mankind, especially the Americans.

"When I was a kid, my parents took me to visit Mexico City. I'll always remember my father's attitude – boisterous, boastful. And my mother didn't like the locals because they were swarthy [...] And I can see my father and mother landing on Mars and behaving the same way" (page 109).

The charge is scathing, without half measures, and can easily be compared to other criticisms, such as the more underlying one of the *American way of life*, parodied in the description of the Martian couple in the short story "Ylla", or the more ironic one of the bureaucratic inculture that censors for fear of the unknown, and bans Edgar Allan Poe's books without ever having read them (in the short story "Usher II").

In the same short story "...And the Moon That Shines", Bradbury also makes his views on the Martian question explicit, through the voice of the character Cheroke:

> "I have Cherokee blood in my veins. My grandfather told me all about Oklahoma and the Indian Territory. If there's a Martian around, I'm all for him" (page 103).

Bradbury does not hesitate to criticise the very foundations of the American nation, and thus the national identity of his main readership, by exposing the issue of genocide. The Martians have almost disappeared from the surface of their planet, having died of chicken pox, innocently brought by previous explorers, thus leaving the way open for the massive arrival of immigrants, compared to locusts. In the end, the novel describes a true transposition from America to Mars, without adjustments:

> "In many ways, you would have thought that a huge earthquake had uprooted a town in Iowa, and that in an instant a cyclone the size of the Land of Oz had carried it as it was to Mars and deposited it there without a tremor" (page 170).

However, Mars is also seen as a possible solution to man's problems on Earth, and specifically that of segregation, in the short story "Up There in the Sky". This story, centred on the character of the hardware dealer Sam Teece, with his revolting language ('that stupid nigger', page 188, or 'kill that son of a bitch', page 202), tells the story of the departure of blacks from the southern United States to Mars from the point of view of a racist white man.

The irony of the story is, of course, in the white man's despair, unable not to feel both envy and resentment at this exile – in his view, the black population should not be allowed to leave without his permission, and Mars should remain a promise to men like him.

The pathetic attitude of Teece, who will do anything to prevent this departure (even invoking a debt of fifty dollars and a contract ending in a month), makes it possible to clearly identify America's ambivalent attitude towards blacks at the turn of the 1950s – if they treat them brutally, they cannot do without them. Bradbury's point is clear, and again, scathing. Here, Mars is no longer used as a mirror to illuminate the unbearable colonizing attitude of the Americans, but reflects the unhealthy state of their society at the time of the novel's publication. The historical charge turns into a social critique.

However, not everything in Bradbury's relationship with America is negative, and there is a real melancholy of the homeland in the novel. This unfolds in the novella "The Third Expedition", when the explorers are surprised to arrive on Mars in a mid-2000s Illinois hamlet and find all their relatives gone. But in the end, the novel's deep melancholy lies in its resolution – when these rude Americans, who have only made Mars ugly, prefer to return to Earth to die with their fellow human beings rather than continue to live without them, thus demonstrating, in the end, a profound and unexpected humanity.

A PACIFIST AND HUMANIST NOVEL

The Martian Chronicles present a pessimistic, almost fatalistic vision of the future – published at the end of the Second World War, the short stories evoke from time to time the interminable wars on Earth, and the outbreak in November 2036 of a total, final war, to the point that the planet is set ablaze in the starry sky of Mars: "The Australian continent atomised. Los Angeles, London, bombed. War" (page 267).

Mars has a double symbolic role in this respect: on the one hand, the possibility of escape and new beginnings; on the other, the example of a successful society. The first possibility seems to be negated at first when the colonists, still too recently arrived, decide to return to Earth to join humanity in peril, but is finally fully activated in the last story, "Picnic in a Million Years", when a family manages to flee Earth and reach Mars in the hope of founding a new humanity, of giving it a second chance. This is a true science fiction topos, a culmination prepared by the succession of short stories that underline, in a hollow way, how the failed colonisation constitutes a waste of the possibilities offered by the planet.

More interesting is Bradbury's willingness to evoke, in sporadic touches, Martian society as a model to follow – first in opposition to the American settler, but ultimately (again), as a goal to be achieved by the new humanity, in a magnificent move that makes the last survivors of Earth the first Martians:

"I've always wanted to see a Martian," said Michael. "Where are they, Dad? You promised." "Here they are," said Dad. He hoisted Michael onto his shoulder and pointed down. The Martians were there. Timothy shivered. The Martians were there – in the canal – reflected in the water. Timothy, Michael, Robert, Mom and Dad. The Martians looked back at them for a long, long moment of silence in the ripples of the water..." (page 318, excipit of the novel).

These last lines embody a tension that runs through all the stories, between Man who fails in his relationship with the world and the Martian who has achieved a balance with his environment – in other words, between real Man and Man as he should be according to Bradbury, real Man, endearing, detestable, full of faults, and ideal Man, impossible.

"They knew how to combine art with life. For Americans, it's always been a separate thing. Something that is relegated to the top room, the room of the family idiot. Something you take a dose of on Sundays, with the occasional shot of religion. Among the Martians, everything coexists, art, religion and everything else" (page 109), says Spender. "Once we were men with bodies, legs and arms like you. According to legend, one of us, a good man, discovered a way to free the human soul and intellect, to free us from physical ailments and melancholy, from death and change, from bad temper and senility" (page 167), explain the fireballs that Father Peregrine would like to free from sin. Bradbury thus defends another vision of the world, of man – he does not only criticise, he proposes an alternative.

Ray Bradbury extends this humanistic painting through the Martians and the few characters who understand them to the planet, to the beauty of the landscapes and the abandoned cities, described with restraint and poetry, leaving the reader to his imagination. The author also adopts an environmentalist stance that is far ahead of its time, contrasting the Earth of factories with a prodigiously fertile Mars. Spender's speech ("We Earthlings have a gift for ruining beautiful things"(page 96), or "Isn't it enough for them to have destroyed a planet? Do they have to pollute other people's feeders too? Poor brainless baudruches' (page 110), is thus to be read in parallel with the short story "The Green Morning", where thousands of trees grow in one night, 'nourished by a foreign and magical soil' (page 128). If individual humans can achieve good, humanity as a species can only be a poison to its environment, like the character of Sam Parkhill in the short story "The Off-Season" the archetypal self-centred egotist who only sees ways to improve his own situation.

FOOD FOR THOUGHT

A FEW QUESTIONS TO DEEPEN YOUR REFLECTION...

- The text seems devoid of any scientific reflection on the feasibility of space travel to Mars and the possibility of extraterrestrial life. What aesthetic effect does this create?

- When originally published, the stories were set between 1999 and 2026. The 1997 reprint pushed the dates more than thirty years into the future. Why is this? Does the reader really believe, in 1950 as today, that the future of the novel is a possible future?

- Bradbury likes to take a hard line - against racism, censorship, religion or sexism. Which short stories do you find most effective in dealing with such issues?

- Can you easily distinguish between the original short stories, published separately, and the texts written especially for the novel? How can you do this?

- Bradbury exclaims in his preface, "Don't tell me what I'm doing; I don't want to know!" How can this quote accompany your reading of the novel?

- Several times in *The Martian Chronicles*, the reader finds himself in a position to identify with murderous characters. Which ones? How does Bradbury achieve this?

- While most of the stories have a proper ending, some seem to ask for a sequel, which is never given, or is given in a lapidary way. Which story would you like to continue? Just imagine.

- Speaking of *The Martian Chronicles*, Bradbury says that it is not science fiction, but rather compares his text to Greek myths. What does he mean by this?

TO GO FURTHER

REFERENCE EDITION

Chroniques martiennes, translated from English by Jacques Chambon and Henri Robillot, Paris, Denoël, 2001, 318 p.

BENCHMARK STUDIES

SAINT-GELAIS, R., *L'Empire du pseudo*, Québec, Les Éditions Nota bene, 1999, 400 p.

ADDITIONAL SOURCES

BRADBURY, R., *Fahrenheit 451*, translated from English by Jacques Chambon and Henri Robillot, Paris, Denoël, 1995, 288 p.

ASIMOV, I., *Fondation*, translated from English by Jean Rosenthal, Paris, Denoël, 1966, 251 p.

ADAPTATIONS

In 1966, the novel was adapted for the stage by director Louis Pauwels, with Jean-Louis Barrault among others.

In 1974, a French TV film directed by Renée Kammerscheit was based on the adaptation by Louis Pauwels.

In 1980, the novel was adapted as a three-part television film, directed by Michael Anderson from a screenplay by Richard Matheson (a great name in American science fiction, famous for *I Am Legend*, 1954, and *The Shrinking Man*, 1956), starring Rock Hudson.

A great many short stories have been adapted separately for television or short films, as well as for other media, such as comics.

Your opinion is important to us!
Leave a comment on the website of your online bookshop
and share your favourites on social networks!

www.brightsummaries.com

Ebook EAN: 9782808686655
Paperback EAN: 9782808698054
Legal Deposit: D/2023/12603/1085

Cover: © Primento
Digital conception by Primento, the digital partner of publishers.

Printed in Great Britain
by Amazon

28818965R00020